DELICATE THOUGHTS

M. BALLARD

Delicate Thoughts
a collection of poetry and prose written by M. Ballard

Printed in the United States of America

Cover Design: TreManda Pewett
Editor: Carla DuPont Huger
Illustration: TreManda Pewett

ISBN 13: 978-0-9974265-9-5
ISBN 10: 0-9974265-9-4

Jeanius Publishing LLC
430 Lee Blvd
Lehigh Acres, FL 33936

For more information, please visit:
Jeaniuspublishing.com

DELICATE THOUGHTS

M. BALLARD

eanius
PUBLISHING

to the ones who thought they broke us.

somewhere between the ages of 18 and 23

i decided to starve myself thin

and make a home out of men

that's when it all starts

that's when the downfall begins.

Delicate Thoughts

part 1

drowning

raw.

hello, my dear

this is so wrong, my dear

i know i shouldn't be writing you, but i've been

drinking and i've been up for way too long, my dear

you've been running around in my mind, my dear

the tears have dried but the scars persist

the crack in my heart,

 the scars you left behind, my dear

made me feel guilty for things i shouldn't do

made me feel guilty for the things you did, too

you said you were sorry, "i'm stubborn, can i come

over?"

i said, "i forgive you, my dear"

you stay until daylight hits and i ask you, "when will

i see you again?" you reply, "soon."

soon.

well i haven't seen you, my dear

why did you lie, my dear?

the cuts on my heart get deeper as i call your phone

Delicate Thoughts

and get no reply,

my dear

i thought you were kind, my dear

i thought you were "mine," my dear

was she special enough to know your middle name?

did she crack the code?

did she find the key to your heart that i've been

frantically searching for,

for a year, my dear?

i was in love with you, should i have made that more

clear, my dear?

all the arguing and fighting had gotten to you

i couldn't stop, i knew i was testing it

but if it's not in God's plan for us to be together, then

who am I to question it?

now tell me after all of this, was i worth the long

drive, my dear?

i doubt you'll read this, but i'll send it anyway

just so you know

my heart is still beating

and i'm still alive, my dear.

why

when you open up that mouth of yours
flowers pour out
and i believed every beautiful word you said
if you knew i fall in love so easily
like falling asleep comes at night
you wouldn't have done this to me
 now the memory of your lips on mine
burn like that first sip of alcohol,
because i know everything you
said to me was a lie

Delicate Thoughts

fragile

when i look at you, i see someone i could spend
forever with
someone i could sit out on the porch with when we
are gray
and talk about when we were young
someone who would be there for me when i was sick
make me soup, and tuck me into bed
someone who i would give my heart to
and remember; it is fragile, so please handle it with
care

when you look at me, you see a girl who is naive and
broken
someone who would melt like putty in your hands
when you whisper sweet words into her ear
someone who you could sink your body into
whenever you wanted to
because she trusts you
and when she falls in love and she gives you her
soul,
but you only want her body
you leave
and she is heartbroken
her heart is fragile,
and you forgot to handle it with care

Delicate Thoughts

oct 23rd

the smell of your cologne reminds me of hope and
heartbreak,
                    and i want it all over me

blame

how do you do it
find a way to turn everything on me
you could stab me straight in the heart
and tell me to be more careful next time
nothing is ever your fault

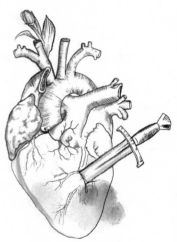

Delicate Thoughts

selfish

and you wanted me all to yourself,
but you didn't want to give all of yourself to me
how selfish could you be

time.

come lay with me
on my soft satin sheets
kiss my collarbones,
as we slowly fall asleep
and drift off
into the milky way galaxy

Delicate Thoughts

caution

who knew you'd end up being

   my biggest trigger warning

      the very thought of you

         makes me go *insane*

note to self: if you tell them you write poems and they don't ask to see your work, then they do not plan on staying in your life. for poems are the best way of getting to know someone else, inside and out.

Delicate Thoughts

fool

you gave me your lies wrapped up all nicely
 with a big beautiful bow
i cried
you apologized
i forgave

          you did it again

curiosity

i'd love to delve into the inner-workings of your mind
i know it's a dark place and i might get lost
 but i'm willing to risk it

Delicate Thoughts

illusions

lipstick makes her look put together

when she smiles that lipstick smile

they don't know the pain

that she's been through

almost more than she could take

if only they knew

that her lipstick smile is fake

chaos

i remember your eyes would light up

every time you'd see me

you would kiss my feet

you would move heaven and earth for me

but eventually that light in your eyes became dull

and you stopped treating me like someone

and started treating me like anyone

i wish i could pinpoint

that exact moment i went from your world,

to just another girl

Delicate Thoughts

dec 10th

it's been days since we last spoke
 and my heart skips a beat
every time my phone rings
i'd rather argue with you all night
            than to never hear from you at all

pain

you looked at her with a brightness i was familiar
with
you touched her softly like you used to touch me
your hand fit so perfectly around her waist just like
mine

but when you spoke her name
 the edges of your lips curled into a smile
that i had never seen before

Delicate Thoughts

honey

the sound of your voice
reminds me of soft dripping water
how do you say the most horrible things
and make them sound beautiful

M. Ballard

karma

i could destroy you if i wanted to
like you destroyed the walls around my heart
and beat your way in
but i won't let my anger win
instead i'll let it go,
and hope that one day your future daughter
brings home someone
                    just like you

Delicate Thoughts

restart

i was always so afraid of love and getting hurt
until i met you
and the world was so beautiful
and i didn't feel so afraid anymore

but then you broke me
now i'm right back to where i started

M. Ballard

how to lose your mind:

1. give your heart, mind, soul and body to someone.
give it all away until there is nothing left inside you.
2. let them feed you all of their equivocations and
half-baked promises. keep going until your stomach
aches.
3. pray that they stay. and despite all of the signs that
they are not right for you, give yourself false hope. it
is the only thing you have left.
4. when they start to get distant, light a candle, watch
it burn down to the wick, and wait
on a call that never comes.
5. close your eyes and count to ten. this is when it
starts to hurt.
6. try to piece yourself back together. give them all
the things that they've left, and kiss them goodbye.
(remember not to lick your lips, because the
aftertaste is never sweet)

Delicate Thoughts

hypocrisy

don't look at me that way

with those judgmental eyes

and don't you *ever* question my intentions for you

      when yours were never pure for me

M. Ballard

young

years have passed, seasons have alternated, and the day has shifted into night, yet the thought of you has not shifted at all. you introduced me to a fairytale kind of love that i thought was only in novels i used to read as an adolescent. you never accepted failure when it came to the matter of my laughter. we'd laugh until our vocal cords protested. even though we were young, we were never childish; only child-like. we'd run after each other into the night, as if one of us held the sun. in a world so obviously tainted, your smile was my only guiding light.

Delicate Thoughts

burn

i could start a forest fire
with all the anger
you have created inside of me

M. Ballard

unsettled

kiss my forehead and tell me i'm pretty

that is all i want

wipe my tears away

tell me everything will be okay

i hope that you don't get offended when i tell you

that i wish i didn't need you

because you are part of the reason

that i am so broken in the first place

but when i am in your arms

you are the glue to piece me back together,

and i hate that you know just what to say

to break me apart again

(you are the cause, but you are also the remedy.)

Delicate Thoughts

abandonment

i don't check out books from the library anymore
i just buy them
because i'm very bad at giving up things that i love
that's why i still hold onto you

M. Ballard

april 1st

one. last. false. belief.
you always sound convincing
april fools' to me

Delicate Thoughts

note to self: block his number

M. Ballard

2 a.m.

maybe it's because i'm lonely right now
or maybe it's because this water i'm drinking
tastes a lot like vodka
maybe it's a combination of both

but the thought of me in your arms tonight
sounds a lot like paradise

Delicate Thoughts

grace

you could break my heart a million and one times,
and i'll still run back to you
i guess what i'm trying to say is:
i am the church, and you are my religion

poison

we spewed venom out of our mouths to hurt one
another
we did it so much until we eventually hurt ourselves,
and had no choice but to let go

-toxic relationships

Delicate Thoughts

nocturnal

at night i stay up sighing loudly

      trying to rid you from my chest

M. Ballard

gemini

you were as sweet as saccharine

but you were mean when you wanted to be

you used to love when i wore those tight little

dresses, so when you were around i always wore one,

hoping it'd make you love me

but eventually it stopped working

i guess i lost my touch

i guess you stopped caring

i guess over time we both had lost our minds

you: for breaking me down and making me feel

worthless

me: for staying and hoping it'd get better

(*it never did.*)

Delicate Thoughts

capricorn

hey it's me again
sorry to bother you
i'm currently writing this letter from my grave
because you killed me
a lot of my writing is about you,
and you know that
you were the one i trusted the most
and i think when you left
you took a part of me with you
it might have been my soul

M. Ballard

note to self: you exist in all that exists

Delicate Thoughts

refuge

i am not your shelter
i am not just a vessel you can enter
for temporary warmth
don't make a home out of me
if you don't intend to stay

M. Ballard

betrayal

the mind is a powerful thing, let me tell you. i've been
doing so good at disconnecting myself from you, but
last night i had a dream that you texted me. and the
worst part about it, was that i knew i was dreaming. i
was fully aware that the dream version of you was
contacting me, and i still let it continue. i knew i was
dreaming because i know you well enough that you'd
never contact me if i didn't contact
you first.

but the dream version of you still wanted me as much
as the real me wanted you. it's funny how you could
want something so bad, that your mind could
manifest it.
the mind is a powerful thing, let me tell you. no
matter how much you try to block someone out, your
soul knows they're still inside you. they come to you
in your dreams and when you wake up, they leave

Delicate Thoughts

you to clean up the mess they made. how could your
mind betray you like that? the mind is a powerful
thing, let me tell you.

M. Ballard

complications

when we first met

i thought you were a tall glass of water

that i wanted to drink

but you ended up being

just a shot glass of whiskey

that left a bitter taste in my mouth

Delicate Thoughts

evocative

limbs entangled
lips swollen from kisses
you saw the photo i sent to you titled,
"for your eyes only"

you came over for passion,
midnight's secrecy
i know this isn't love
but let's pretend for the night
as i lay in your embrace

M. Ballard

skin

we were so beautiful

our black/white skin

i imagined us being together forever

with our black/white kids

scaring the people who still lived

like there were black/white TVs

i imagined us turning our heads

 and laughing

at how appalled they were

if only they knew, in our minds

we were colorblind

and when they saw us smiling

they'd be jealous

and wish they had something like us,

and slowly they'd start to envy

                    our black/white love

Delicate Thoughts

insecure

hey, i haven't heard from you
we were supposed to chill again
i hope i didn't scare you off
i hope you didn't see the insecurities written on my
face
weren't you impressed by my smile
my walk
the dip of my waist

i laughed at all your stupid jokes
i even complimented your hair
not sure why i haven't heard from you
you said you wanted to see this through
you said i was smart
you said i was different than the others

i guess i'll cross you off the list

and place you in the box

with all my other potential lovers

M. Ballard

vice

we both know why you're here
you know i couldn't help inviting you over
i'm an addict and you are my vice
i know i need to let go, but i needed one last fix
 before i scrubbed myself clean of you

Delicate Thoughts

scorpio

remember when we'd laugh all night
remember when we'd look up at the sky
 and talk about our future
i never really knew what hazel eyes looked like
until i looked into yours
and now hazel eyes are my favorite

i can't say anything bad about you
and maybe that's why we didn't last
because you were too good
and i always wanted bad

(i need someone that needs fixing as much as i need

fixing myself.)

M. Ballard

lolita

i was your little secret

a man twice my age,

twice my wit

i was your beautiful, helpless little damsel

and you always came to save the day

as months passed you were

stretched so thin between your family and me

that you eventually became invisible

and you were never seen again

Delicate Thoughts

february 14th

say something sweet to me

to get me through the day

M. Ballard

confessional

my belly ached and i was always hungry for you, waiting for you to fill me up.

you filled me up physically--but emotionally, that was a different story. we were bad at communicating, but we excelled at making love. i used to make excuses for you, i used to tell myself to, "give him some time." i used to tell myself it would get better. you knew me so differently. you knew me better than anyone ever could. you knew about my depression, and one time we sat and traded

horror stories about all the times we tried to hurt ourselves.

don't you ever tell.

i wish i could take back those secrets from you--i wish i could pull them out of you, and put them in a safe place with a lock and a key.

you didn't deserve to know me like that.

you didn't deserve to know me like i knew me.

Delicate Thoughts

honey, don't you know that i loved you without
condition?

i loved you when you ignored me, i loved you when
you hurt me. i loved you even after that time i spent
my rent money on those tickets, only for you to flake
on me.

you said it was for family reasons, but baby you
never made it up to me. i guess i know the truth now.
 i guess i know why you did it.

why did i keep on forgiving you? because your love
was the only love i knew,
and i got comfortable being mistreated by you.
i was too busy trying to build a house in a hurricane
to realize you had already gone away.
but i do miss laying with you and tracing my
fingers across your tattoos.

i would ask you what you wanted to watch--you
always let me choose. i miss the way that you looked
at me and the way you always muttered under your

breath that i was beautiful.

i guess i made the mistake of not telling you how much you meant to me. but i thought you already knew it by the way i always let you back into my heart, or the way that i would always text you that i missed you when we were apart.

we could've spoken life into each other and let our love bloom.

but instead, you let it wilt.

we could've been so beautiful.

Delicate Thoughts

advenire

you held a kind of uncertainty
that was always intriguing to me
like space and planets and heaven
you don't know exactly what it holds
but you still want to explore every inch of it

M. Ballard

cold

oh, honey

i moved the mountains

and the sun

and the moon for you

i saw heaven in your eyes

you warmed my soul all through the winter

but as summer arrived

the sun came out

i unthawed,

and you became distant

Delicate Thoughts

pillow-talk

the way you hesitated
when i asked if you missed me
was enough for me to realize
       that i was done trying to make it work

M. Ballard

cravings

you see, everybody needs love
  but some need it more than others
    to balance out the darkness inside them
      they need something they can hold onto
        they need something to keep them going

Delicate Thoughts

melancholy

i keep thinking back to the first few weeks we met
each other,
and how well you treated me
i remember when you took me to a baseball game
and you bent down to tie my shoe so i wouldn't fall
i bet you didn't know that i had already fell
i fell for you
you held so much promise
we held so much promise
those are the sweet memories i will forever cherish

M. Ballard

volumes

and i know you said nothing
but nothing spoke volumes
more than any words ever could

Delicate Thoughts

fire

so now that some time has passed, it hurts a little less
but that doesn't mean i still don't burn
at the sound of your name

M. Ballard

forever

forever is a long time

forever stretches on to eternity

all the oceans put together couldn't describe how long

forever is

we could *never* fathom how long forever is

forever has no number

forever has no end

forever means until the universe is dark and nothing

else is left,

including the stars that burn in the sky for billions

and billions of years

so when i said i'd love you forever,

close your eyes and picture all of those things,

and it still wouldn't compare to how deep,

how vast,

how big

my love was-- *is* for you.

Delicate Thoughts

abuse

i was once told that the tongue is a mighty sword
and honey, yours was powerful
you never put a finger on me
you only hurt me with your words
but no one cares
unless there are bruises to show
no one cares unless you are bloody and broken on the
outside
emotional abuse is the same as physical,
probably even worse

(it takes longer to heal. i'm still healing.)

M. Ballard

mischance

we were two stubborn souls
both broken
trying to come together
as a whole
let's face it honey
we were doomed from the start

Delicate Thoughts

magic

your hands
    and your eyes
        pulled everything out of me
            secrets i had kept buried for years,
                unearthed
                    when you touched me

M. Ballard

depression

some nights i find solace in being alone

other nights i just need somebody at night to hold me

to make me feel something

that's the thing with depression,

you never know where it will take you

depression is pushing and pulling

depression is lowercase letters

and blank spaces

      and unfinished sentences

Delicate Thoughts

clarity

the way that you looked at me i knew

there was no hope there

and i think that's what broke me

to see that there was nothing left of me in you

when you were still in me

i guess now i need to set you free

M. Ballard

spirited

love is not an emotion
it is a being of its own
hiding in the creases of our smiles
and the space between our fingertips

it's the blood in our veins
the steady thump in our hearts

it's the buzzing sound you hear
when you're in a silent room
alone with your thoughts

Delicate Thoughts

secrecy

my eyes tell the stories

    that i can never form into words

        so look at me

          and listen carefully

M. Ballard

part 2

flying

Delicate Thoughts

free

she was everything

oh my god she was everything

she was like a butterfly

so beautiful

so hard to catch

she didn't want to be locked up

he tried to hold her down

but she broke free

she will never be his,

because she's too busy

being her own

note to self: become so invincible, so confident,

so unbelievably strong,

that no one can tell you who you are.

- un b o t h e r e d

Delicate Thoughts

endings

i have grown tired of trying
 to keep your attention
and fighting for your affection
if i'm not enough to keep your heart still
then i shall set you free
if my love doesn't move you to tears
then please let me be

M. Ballard

relinquish

my lungs filled with smoke
and it was too late once i finally realized
 that you were the fire
so now i will learn to let go
and once i do
my lungs will clear
and i will learn to breathe
again

Delicate Thoughts

note to self:

recognize your greatness,

continue to prosper

M. Ballard

goddess

why do us women cry over these men
who are not worthy of our love
why should we burn for these men
who have no intentions
of putting our fire out

Delicate Thoughts

waves.

sadness, happiness, depression, anxiety,

it all comes and goes in waves

i'm learning to deal with it all

and trying my best not to drown in these emotions

it's a fighting game with yourself

when you are so beautifully broken

M. Ballard

grow

you didn't love me
you only loved parts of me
and the longer you stayed gone
i learned to love all of the parts of me
that you neglected

Delicate Thoughts

lessons

if only you knew how many times i've woken up in
the middle of the night
and reached for you, only to realize you weren't there
if only you knew how many times i've cried in public
at just the thought of you
mascara-stained tears that i could wipe away
but those memories, they always stay
if only you knew how long it took me to find myself
if only you knew how many times i struggled
just to get up on my feet

if only you knew how much you inspired me
if only you knew you lit a fire under me
this isn't to be pitied
this isn't to make me feel better
this is just a poem for you,
to say thank you
for helping shape me into who i am today

heal

writing has become my therapy
with every word i write
i am becoming stronger
i am healing myself
with my own words

Delicate Thoughts

hope.

she is someone who is afraid to open up
because once she did, her heart was broken
but she must learn that there will be light
at the end of the tunnel
one day she will find her light,
shining bright upon her,
warming her face and finally,
finally, she will crack a smile

M. Ballard

feign

i don't count the days i've last seen you anymore
i don't write your name in my journal like i used to
and you've stopped coming to me in my dreams

i put all my time and dedication into loving you,
but in the process
i ended up losing myself

nectar

even after years have passed

i know you will lay in bed next to your lover

and my name will still be on the tip of your tongue

threatening to slip out of your lips

i know that you'll miss me

fixing you with my love

contentment

it's ok if you don't got me,

        because *i got me*

            more than anyone ever could

Delicate Thoughts

power

the stretch marks on your thighs are battle wounds

from being a woman

and you should not be ashamed of them

because us women

we are soft creatures

but we are strong

M. Ballard

women

you are a woman
the universe was made of you
without woman there would be no man
remember that when you feel worthless
you are oxygen
you are earth
you are the galaxy
the moon
and the stars
and without those things,
life would cease to exist
you are woman
                    the universe is you

Delicate Thoughts

matter

they are not worth your time if

they make excuses for their actions

instead of owning up to them

M. Ballard

golden

i'm starting to think my melanin was too much for
you
you couldn't handle my bee stung-lips
you couldn't handle that i could start wars with these
hips
i was too much for you
tell me how it feels to know that you cheated yourself
by giving up a goddess
you hated the challenge
so you ran to something comfortable,
but i'm confident enough to love me for the both us

honey, i'm golden.

the biggest mistake you can make,

is underestimate the power of a woman

note to self: don't ever fully give yourself to any man
unless he proves he is worthy--
over
and over again.

(and even when he does, leave some of yourself for
you.)

Delicate Thoughts

peace

have some respect for yourself girl
i know it seems difficult
but all you have to do is put one foot
in front of the other,
and just walk away

M. Ballard

wonder

don't you know that there's someone better right
around the corner
waiting patiently on you to heal so you can find
them?

Delicate Thoughts

forgiveness

on tough nights like these when i stay up all night
thinking of you,
i can do either one of two things:

either i can fall to the ground and beat my fists on the
pavement
until my hands are bloody and broken
and scream to the sky asking what i did to deserve
this
scream until my voice gets hoarse and cry until there
are no tears left and my body shakes with sadness,

or

i can smile, and i can forgive you,
and thank you for being there for me
when nobody else was
i can think about the good times
and i can accept the fact that you were only

meant to be in my life for a short moment in time
and i can remember the feeling you used to give me
and find that feeling within myself
and in that moment,
 i know that i have finally found inner peace
you're so amazing
you're so great
i know that you broke me
and i know you only did it
because you were broken yourself,
but just know that
                    i forgive you

Delicate Thoughts

and i'm sorry i hurt you,
i'm sorry we hurt each other.

M. Ballard

masterpiece

my worth is not defined by the amount
of attention men give me
i am a work of art regardless

Delicate Thoughts

to my future lover:

there's something holding me back from loving you fully…maybe it's my insecurities and me being afraid, that you won't love me back the way i love you. i held my ex-lover in my bones, and i made the mistake of giving myself away too quickly before i had any reassurance.

i'm afraid that if i love you too hard i might scare you away, because my love is a hurricane; mighty and big, and too much to handle. if i give you myself, you have to understand that i don't hold back. it might get scary at times, but i promise you will be happy. i will hold you down like no other,

that is a promise.

M. Ballard

to whom it may concern:

my eyes burn from lack of sleep, but i needed to get up and write this to remind you that you are worth something. i know you may feel disposable, but you are one in a million, and the night the stars aligned and you were created was not a mistake, and if no one told you they loved you today and you've been feeling unappreciated lately just know that you are not alone and i love you. please don't do anything stupid. you are beautiful. you are worth more than diamonds and gold. wherever you are in the world, just know i would climb the highest mountaintop to yell that to you so you could hear it, and hopefully you'd receive it.

Delicate Thoughts

cope

i was blessed and cursed with this gift of writing
in a way that is so raw that it pulls out emotions
inside of me
old memories are made new and i'm forced to lick my
wounds
but i continue to write because even though it hurts,
it somehow makes it all better

M. Ballard

may 1st

but don't you know that there's so much hope inside
me that i am bursting at the seams
despite the wrong that has been done to me?

my life holds so much promise

and i know that i am often sad
and get so wrapped up in my own thoughts i forget to
breathe, but i need to remember that God gave me
all this oxygen in my lungs for a reason
i guess what i'm trying to say, is i will be okay
so please,
please be patient with me.

Delicate Thoughts

progress

i am the product of my mother and father,
and the relatives who came before them
soft spoken
hard to impress
easily bruised insides encased in an exterior of brown
skin
encased in a little black dress

i am the product of everyone i've ever loved
and everyone who loved me

the words of past lovers who whispered
broken promises
and sweet nothings in my ear are permanently burned
into my head,
and the traces of their fingertips
are permanently etched onto my body
i am the product of my father and mother
and past lovers,

for they have made me who i am today

i am emotional

i am messy

i am weak and strong both at the same time

i am a work in progress.

Delicate Thoughts

deliverance

i know you often feel mistreated
and i know that the darkness of the world
sometimes gets to you,
but everything is better with a hot lavender bath
coconut oil
and the work of the Lord
take my hand, queen
and let's get through this together

M. Ballard

divinity

you are a sight for sore eyes my dear

you are a flower blooming in the spring

    and your smile is light in a too dim world

Delicate Thoughts

onward.

i learned that changing yourself won't make him love
you
you could lose weight, shave every inch of your
body,
grow your hair long, please him and give him
everything he's ever wanted,
scratch his name into every bone, like ink into skin--
but my darling, *this won't work*

i waited all night for his voice to wrap me in comfort
and reassurance
and when it never came, i realized i didn't need
affirmations; i needed confidence
you could do everything in your power to make them
stay,
but if they don't love you,
they will still leave

and *let them leave*

M. Ballard

because my darling, you are special
you are for someone, don't ever change.

Delicate Thoughts

galaxygirl

she's the type of girl that when you look at her, you
know she will be somebody someday. she is born to
be successful. she walks with a stride, she moves
quickly on her feet. no one ever calls her slow. no
one ever calls her lazy. when she walks by, men stare
at her with stars in their eyes. they try to get her, but
she's quick-- *catch her if you can.*
she's one of those girls who are often quiet, but when
she speaks, she does it with purpose. and best believe
when she has something to say, everyone listens.

she is the epitome of unattainable. she is the epitome
of grace. she has a lion heart, but her head is a junk
drawer full of emotions and if you empty it out, you'll
see all the mess she is holding. and despite this, she is
still keeping it together.
when you look at her exterior, you see someone who
knows where life is taking her. but in reality, she is
taking life day by day, just trying to find a reason to

get up out of bed and look presentable enough for the world. but she does it, every single day. she finds something to live for. she smiles through that pain because she knows that *this too shall pass*, and she'll be who she is truly meant to be someday.

if this describes you, we are one and the same.

Delicate Thoughts

pride

with fire in my heart

and a twinkle in my eye,

i smile

as i confidently say this:

break me down, and watch me

build myself up stronger than before.

gratitude

i hope that when i leave this world, i leave some kind
of impact
on at least one person who has been in my life
if not, i thank you anyway for helping me turn my
sadness,
and frustrations,
and realizations
into a beautiful piece of art.

Delicate Thoughts

epilogue

I've always loved reading poetry, but I never thought I was talented enough to actually write it. I was always someone who wrote fiction novels for young adults. I loved creating characters and the storyline and the plot, I loved that I could be the one to make up a whole new world, and I still do. It wasn't until recently did I realize that I could actually use my own life and my heartbreak and struggles, and turn them into a piece of art.

Starting October of 2016, I started to write down my thoughts and poems in the Notes app on my phone, documenting every emotion I was feeling. I realized that I was always someone who was better at writing down my thoughts and feelings instead of saying them in the moment. Some would say it was a curse, but I think it's a blessing.

I know there are other poets out there that are better

at writing than me, that know how to create beautifully formed sentences that could bring anyone to tears. But I'm not them, I'm me. And all I can do is tell my story in the best way that I know, and hope that someone out there can take these words in this book and find some kind of solace in them. I hope these words bode well with you, and I hope you feel them as intensely as I did as I was writing them. I hope these words help you in some way. I hope these words nourish your soul.

National Suicide Prevention Lifeline

1-800-273-8255

You can get in touch with M. Ballard at

Email: mballardwrites@gmail.com

Instagram: @mballardwrites

Facebook: M. Ballard

Made in the USA
San Bernardino, CA
06 November 2017